Stiletto

II

By Azaan Kamau

Stiletto II

Published by Glover Lane Press
(424)703-3277
gloverpublishing@gmail.com
www,Facebook.com/Gloverlanepress

Copyright © 2023 by Azaan Kamau and
Jennifer M. Glover

ISBN: 978-1-7368112-3-8

All right reserved. No part of this book may be reproduced in any form or by electronic or mechanical means without the Written permission of Azaan Kamau and Jennifer M. Glover

Photography, Cover and Design by
Azaan Kamau

azaankamau@gmail.com or
gloverpublishing@gmail.com

For Titles By Azaan Kamau
Visit her on Amazon
www.Facebook.com/gloverlanepress

Thank You

I would like to thank Tara J. Brown for being the Brains!

Thank you to Dr. Michael Beckwith & Teddy Rabbs for being a constant reminder that I can do, and be anything if I believe it!

Ifalade Ta'Shia Asanti, simply put my gratitude has no bounds!

Thank you Ayin Adams who guides me with divine wisdom.

Thank you to the very special Tammie O'Leary.

Thank you so much to the amazing Katrina Arrango for your heart, soul, and all you do!!! Thank you! for all you do!!!

Introduction

My writing has been labeled all sorts of things; taboo, triggering, whimsical, revolutionary, uplifting, informative, educational, and just recently esoteric!

For the first time ever, I have complied a book where the poems are not only erotic, they are downright steamy! Some are explosive!

These is a consistent balance with this poetry book. Of course, there are sexual hair-raising poems, but there is a tiny bit a humor, social issues like abuse, and homophobia.

One of these poems is considered hazardous materials and flammable!

If you love thought provoking, spine-tingling, titillating erotica that leave your panties wet, you will love this book!

EXPLICIT MATERIAL! NOT SUTIBLE FOR MINORS OR THE FAINT OF HEART!

Table of Contents

Daddi Long Stroke 9
Sister Hazel May 12
She Wanted More & More & More 14
Latex Cat Suit 16
Missing You 18
Ripped Fishnets 20
Those Eyes 22
Love Letters 24
Purple Cadillac 26
Lost in Her Eyes 29
Ghetto Girl 32
Biker Babe 35
Yo Shit 37
I'm Psychic 38
The Pussy Whisperer 39
Stiletto 43
Hardwood Floors 46
I Saw You Through the Peephole 47
    About Azaan Kamau 50

Daddi Long Stroke

I would tease her while I leisurely walked toward the Jacuzzi, then sit on the edge with my feet dangling in the hot bubbling water.
My aloof behavior made her more aggressive….more intense.
She had a thirst for sex that was unparalleled, even uncanny.
She got off on watching me attach my thick dong to the leather strap,
she would slowly connect the chrome buckles and snaps with her tongue, then her white teeth.
She purred, are you going to stroke it Daddi?
She would gradually lick the thin strips of leather while she stared me in the eye, waiting,
and watching for my response.
She would beg, and plead. Please Daddi, don't make me beg or it.
I would tease her lips, mouth and tongue with my long and thick 9 inches of cyber skin dick.
I would let her deep throat it for just a moment then forcefully remove it from her mouth.

I would watch her eyes when I snatched it from her.
Her eyes pleaded and begged.
The dildo gradually forced its way into her tight hungry asylum.
Bit by bit, my entire dildo slides into her hungered body.
I watched her flinch and roll her eyes into the back of her head.
I gazed as she grinded and bounced up and down, up and down.
She yelled long stroke it Daddi.
She yelled I love you Daddi Long Stroke as I rode it hard and deep,
raw and harsh, then deep, then shallow.
She moaned and shivered, as her sweaty body slipped and slid against my clutching hands.
Our stomachs slapped and smacked while sweat dripped and slipped.
She yelled as the headboard pounded the walls and chipped the paint.
The loud banging of wood and wall was quickly drowned out by her passion filled shouts...
Long stroke me Daddi
I licked and sucked her full breast while I stroked and rode. She jerked and twitched,

moaning with each deep thrust, stroke it Daddi, stroke me deep Daddi.
Long stroke me Daddi.
I flipped her over to her knees. I pounded her deliberate and deep.
I listened to the moist sloppy sound of her deep sticky opening.
I watched her naked shimmering body, her arched back...
I watched her buck and ride while gripping her waist with my left hand and tickled her clit with my right.
She bellowed as I stroked her swollen steamy clit.
As I pounded my body into hers, I could feel her clit throbbing between my fingers.
As she climaxed, she shivered then squirmed roaring as she erupted the sweetest words...
Daddi, Daddi Long Stroke.
Daddi stoke it, Long Stroke Me Daddi

Sister Hazel May

Each Sunday my only joy came from
sitting next to Sister Hazel May.
I would seek her out before service
began,
I would greet her then hand her a fan and
church bulletin.
She smiled and kissed my cheek leaving
her plum tinted mark on my face.
I beamed as my body felt tingly and
feverish! Every time she felt the spirit,
her floral skirt would fly up revealing her
naked ass, and shaved haven,
her clit was round and thick,
She knew I was craving.
For some reason the buttons on her
salmon-colored blouse would fly off
illuminating black lace.
I would watch her round breast bounce in
her bra while they tried to escape.
I could not resist watching her flop on the
floor with her big thick legs open and
wide.
She would scream "glory", as she wiggled
and trembled, and didn't try to hide.
One time when the spirit was upon her,
she danced right next to me revealing
these honey brown titties,

I tried to get out of the way, but she grabbed me.
Embarrassed and red,
While her full caramel tits slapped and hit me.
I use to love watching her eat.
I would fantasize about her using those full lips to devour me with her tongue and even teeth.
Sister Hazel May had no idea what I use to think,
Now, she only resides in my memories.

She Wanted More & More & More

The room smelled of lilac, while candles danced in the distance.
We listened to the Love Jones soundtrack,
As we reminisced and thought back.
I watched her leisurely unpack cyber-skin, silicone and velcro, harnesses and dildos.
There were piles of sexual knick-knacks; satin blind-folds and long whips, I was a bit sidetracked. There were tubes of lube, latex this and that, silver bullets, vibrators and different sized whips! She smiled and whispered, "just relax!"
We kissed thirsty and deep, the heat from our passion made her wet and slippery.
At some point I was covered with scratches and candle wax.
It seemed as hours passed,
My rhythm was hard, sweltering and fast.
But she still needed more.
She bounced, stroked, and provoked…yet still she needed more & more & more.
The love making was rough then euphoric…but she wanted more.
I watched her move and tremble,
As batteries died and the electricity dwindled,

The lube bottles emptied as velcro and silicone only made her hungry for more...
I thought by now she would have pulled a muscle or maybe she was sore.
She shuddered as she climaxed, then yelled...
I want more!

Latex Cat Suit

Our eyes met as soon as I reached the top of the stairs....
It was 1990 when I first saw her at the Executive Suite.
I was too young to be there, but I didn't care.
I was dressed casual, a polo shirt, Levi's, and freshly braided cornrows.
I was just happy that my ID got through the door!
Her shinny skin tight cat suit hugged and gripped Her body, her thighs, hips and bowed legs.
I thought to myself, "mercy" as I mentally begged.
There were no seams, no zippers, no beginning, just her curves and raw nerve.
I watched her sip her Cosmo, while the music Became falsetto.
I watched her hair move & sway.
I was entranced by her long micro-braids way past her tiny waist.
I watched her movement, it's tempo.
Makin Happy By Crystal Waters vibrato thumped And pounded in the disco.
I focused on her movement and motion that had us all high like a potion.

Everyone watched her.
Their eyes pursued her.
Studs, aggressives, even femme girls in stilettos watched with mouths wide open.
Some rolling their eyes, many just watching her round thighs.
Our eyes met for a brief second, with my face red and flushed.
I was in limbo cuz back then, I had no big ego, nor was I all machismo.
I didn't want her to think I was a weird or some psycho.
I played it off, walked far away to hang with my homie from Frisco.
I had no idea this beautiful woman had followed me,
She tapped me on the shoulder, smiled big and Said hello!
I was startled, then shocked, I dropped my whole bottle of Cisco.

Missing You

As I sit within myself, I feel as if I'm an isolated citadel, alone and void of positive emotion.

I feel like a desert or a raided tomb.

At night it's worse when the utter emptiness consumes.

I feel punished or held hostage when I can't see you, touch you, or breathe you.

I miss your smile.
Warm and loving, soothing and mild.

I miss your massive blue agate necklace, surrounded by silver and other tiny stones.

I miss the look on your face, and the way your eyes twinkle when you smell jasmine.

There are times I feel transported as your lips touch me, devour me.

I can never get enough our unbridled passion, licking biting, sucking, igniting.

I miss your poetic motion, your slow alluring rhythm.

Slow, then hard, fast then violent and filled with aggression, but soft like rose petals.

I miss the way your sweet vanilla sugar perspiration glistens in candlelight.

I thought I knew everything, had all the answers until I met you.

I feel like I'm escaping my grim work day, the monotony by just being in your midst.

I can't even talk to you this lonesome night.

I've looked at your photographs, read your letters and greetings cards.

I've made love to you in my memories.

I'll see you in my dreams, but still I miss you.

Ripped Fishnets

She dangled naked from her fishnets and chandelier.
Ripped fishnets twisted around her wrists,
Legs wide open, wanting, waiting hungrily.
Her eyes growled come get me.
I thought, what the hell, as I was greeted with her intoxicating smell.
Her fragrance made parts of me throb and swell.
My lips touched hers, my skin burned with passion,
I felt untamed, wild and unbridled.
I was on fire as our love making became fucking.
Wild and riot-like as she hung from her ripped fishnets.
I felt lewd and disorderly as I penetrated her starving sacred space.
It purred and smacked while she swallowed my fingers.
She moaned, and yelled filthy slurs and curse words.
She bucked me, while my fingers probed.
I fell to my knees licking and eating her firm abode.
She rode my mouth with a rhythm so illicit,
vile and twisted I felt greedy like a fiend

needing my fix, Willingly I was her hoe, her trick.
The more I ate, her stomach and legs trembled.
She then screamed and bellowed,
I enjoyed watching and tasting her explode.
Who knew her ripped fishnets could hold the weight of our load.

Those Eyes

What is it I see?

Vivid Images flowing freely as if they knew I was watching...

When you are not near, pictures of you flash in my mind.

Laughter and tears, champagne and our golden years.

Her eyes, deep and dark, they are filled with mystery.

Passion of our history written on her face.

Her essence is my strength, boundless, infinite and into forever.

Her eyes teach and speak of the many dynasties of African pain.

Joys of dancing, drumming and singing in the rain.

Her eyes eternal and dark, but filled with light and the fire to press forward.

Those eyes stun and startle me.

They embrace the dark, embracing and illuminating all in her presence.

She melts my fears as she gazes into me.

I become liquid as she touches me just by looking.

Within her eyes, I see my dreams.

I see our future, our meditations materialized....

I see all in within her eyes.

Those eyes,

 I love the way she just sits there and looks into me.

Love Letters

Every time Miki Howard sang to me,
I wrote you a letter.

I would write about your beautiful light
brown eyes, their mystery.
How I loved you beyond all eternity.

I use to think while writing my letters we
would always be.
I never wanted to be your little secret, or
forbidden fantasy.

I always thought it would always be you
and me.
I thought I was too butch.
Too Masculine,
Just too much.

My stud swagga, my boxers, my long
cornrows and sagging jeans.
I use to wonder, was it my stroll, my hair or
just my identity.

Now that I think back, you never really
wanted me,
you were too in fear of your family and
society.

It was your fear of your own sexuality.
My deep and profound love was merely a
casualty.

I had to realize long ago that no matter
the passion in my love letter,
you were never my future or my destiny.

Purple Cadillac

Eager when I opened the door to her penthouse.
Walking down the long dimly lit hall, the sweet scent of plumeria caressed and held me.
I could hear Branford Marsalis blowing his saxophone, as B.B. King chimed in with Lucille.
As I walked into the living room, fresh red rose petals greeted my feet.
Candles flickered in the distance as she slowly emerged from the shadows.
She held a silver wine bucket.
As she came closer, I watched her.
I glanced at the wine bucket which held Blue Curaco, Grenadine and Midori Melon Liquor.
I was a bit puzzled, but I responded with a smile.
She kissed me ever so gently with moist hot lips.
She held my gaze as she led me a pile of pillows near the fireplace.
She unbuttoned my shirt, then removed my belt throwing them both onto the floor.

She unbuttoned, and then unzipped my jeans.
She grinned slow and shy as she removed them from my ankles, then my feet.
I grabbed her and puller her into me.
We kissed hungrily, as she ignited my flame with large searching tongue.
Its wetness made me quiver.
It made me weak.
She froze suddenly searching my eyes....
She poured Blue Curaco in my open mouth until it spilled and dripped from my chin,
Down my chest, then onto my stomach.
Our ferocious kissing had me throb and famished for more.
She then poured Grenadine on my nipples, which dripped and ran down my stomach drenching the front of my underwear.
She sucked, licked and drank my bare shivering flesh while I gasped and moaned.
She then flooded my mouth with sweet Midori Melon Liquor.
As it splashed, spilled and dripped, she licked every inch of me.
She moaned, cum for me my Purple Cadillac, cum for me Baby!

She was drunk as I trembled and
writhed... She insisted on sucking me dry.
She sucked and whispered,
cum for me my Purple Cadillac

Lost in Her Eyes

There I sat.
Alone in the realm of misery
I was lost in the eyes of a woman
Trapped in her web of emotion, deceit, and non-devotion.
Lost, in her eyes.
Lost in the moment.

Her eyes, brown like honey.
Hazel maybe.

They were kind, innocent, and honest.
Eyes angels have!
Sweet, serene, even genuine.
But I was wrong…

The façade faded, but I stayed.
I prayed for the sun to shine, but the storm held its course
I prayed for many things.
A better day, a better way.

Sinister, shady, even wicked.
She wasn't the same woman.
She was different.

Stomped in the dirt, constantly washing my face.
My hands...
Too many tears to count.
Too many promises broken, too many shattered hearts.
Why?
Was my crime just being?
Breathing?

I was lost in the innocents of eyes.
I was their hostage.
Not just my body, but my soul.
Continually told I was stupid, worthless & useless.
I knew better.

But still, all was relinquished to her.
I gave up my being, my joy.
I didn't know who I was, what I liked.
Knowing I was not a conformist, I still conformed.

I lived, constantly in conflict with my being.
I had become someone else, who she wanted me to be.
I went against my grain.
I tried to be who & what she demanded.

I could not, but I tried.

She killed the spirit I tried so hard to kindle.
I died slowly
I was defiled, & persecuted for not being her.
For not having her eyes.
I walked with my head down, a frown on my brow.

I found my way out the maze!
True, many wrong turns were made.
Finally I was free to find my soul I lost so long ago.

Those eyes are etched in my memories.
So innocent, so kind.
When fueled by my independence,
My need for justice,
They radiated their true intent!

Though I fled my misery,
I vowed to myself to never let anyone violate or jail me.

Ghetto Girl

I met her online, she seemed nice enough to meet, and even dine.
She said I'm a lover of life, but I'm a little different.
She liked poetry and long walks,
I thought cool, I'm sure I'll benefit.

I heard bass from a car thumping in the distance, bumping up the street.
I thought to myself, is this who I'm about to meet?

A bright green car came into view, with the most massive rims I have ever seen.
And did I mention the car was neon green?

1983 Chevy Caprice, blasting old school Ice-T;
I thought to myself as the bass vibrated my chest, oh no how can this be?
This old ass Neon Caprice is pulling up to see me!

I could not believe the size of the rims, or the neon blinding green as this young lady appeared from her 1980's machine.

Her smiling pretty face, petite little body emerged from the car wearing a similar shade of neon green!
Thought oh Lord, why me?

Her tiny little body was covered in green, numerous tattoos, and all of her skinny little fingers had a gold ring!
She had the tallest hair I had never seen.
I smiled with joy as she introduced herself, I just couldn't be mean.

Her green halter top exposed her once honey colored flesh, beautiful, creamy and serene.
Every inch of her smooth skin wore a tattoo.
They made her look old, used and quite abused.
Her left cheek, the tops of both hands, her legs and feet were tattooed,
But I guess it all matched her hairdo.

I watched this young lady who was oblivious to my glare, she smiled and blushed as her blinged gold teeth coordinated with her footwear.

I insisted on driving as we left for coffee,

I just couldn't be seen in neon green,
thumping up the street.

She loved theater, poetry, and written
artistry.
She insisted she was not ghetto like others
in her family.

We discussed Sonia Sanchez, Love Poems
and Autumn Blues
As we giggled, people starred at her
tattoos.

She was intelligent, funny, and witty.
I sat enjoying her company,
Watching her secretly.
I wondered to myself, what happened
here, to this dainty little thing?
We became the best of friends while
people would gawk and glare. I use to
think what made her go out in public with
tall green hair?

Biker Babe

She was so young.
She wooed me with her eyes as she
jumped off her chromed bike.
Unzipping her leather jacket,
Her bright red bustier smoldered against
her glowing copper skin.
I gawked at her, her sexy muscular body.
I stared at her leather chaps, the braided
fringe on each leg moved as she glided
toward me.
The massive Coptic cross around her neck
shimmered in the moonlight.
Her tender young skin blended with the
huge Egyptian tattoo on her left arm and
shoulder.
The brilliant hues of red, turquoise and
blue, made me want to rip her clothes off
and expose her.
I was nice and held my composure.
Her bright red lipstick matched her
manicured fingernails.
Did she know how hot she was?
She was so young.
Sometimes she was high, her breath was
dank with Kush.
I didn't care.
I just wanted her moans, her submission,

her gush.
My guilt was all over my face, and behind my eyes when she would shudder then cum.
She was a biker babe!
A young innocent sexy lil femme,
Hungry for the world.
Starving for a gifted stud and hours of great love.
She was wild and free,
She roamed uninhibited and uncontrolled
Yet she hungered to be on her knees,
Pleasing and consuming all of me.
I willingly let her lick and lap me,
ingest then digest me.

Yo Shit

You push my buttons, push me away, pry me, try me.
Embarrass me
Hide me
Pretend your family, parents and friends loathe me
Attend events, go to bars without me
Deny me, then divide me
Constantly lie to me or about me
You are such a phony,
Acting as if you love me
Exhaust my funding
Consume my loving
Crush me, then hump and ride me
Degrade me, invade me
You smile while betraying me
Leave me
Deceive me
Lash me, then wound me
I've had enough of Yo shit, you no longer have the right to use or bruise me.
Please carry on without me!

I'm Psychic

She said allow me to taste you,
Lick you,
Eat you,
Drink and swallow you.
You think you too hard,
You're too butch or
Just too fly?
She said, you don't have a clue how much I want you!
She said allow me to eat it once,
Allow me to kiss it,
Caress and make it lovesick.
Azaan you know I'm psychic,
I know you want it.
Just allow me to taste you,
After a long hard day,
Don't you want me to lap and eat you to soothe and relax you?
Come on Baby, allow me to taste you.

The Pussy Whisperer

Shhhh….

Her body shouted what her lips couldn't.

I listened intensively.

She moaned touch, kiss, and caress me.

Undress me…. slowly.

I kissed her body while her pussy ached for my lips and tongue.

I worshiped her, her needs, the secrets behind her eyes while she laid on her on her back.

She arched her bodice, whined and flinched.

Pinch my nipples, her pussy demanded while her sacred temple called my name.

She elevated her pelvis while bending her knees and spreading her legs.

Shhhh…I understand.

I possess an uncanny skill that I can't deny.

I synced my breathing with hers and stared deep into her eyes.

I can interpret and translate what your place of worship dictates.

Slow, constant and deep….whaaaat you want it nasty, wet and sticky.

I softly kissed her clit in a circular motion, clockwise and counter-clockwise.

Her pussy softly spoke…encircle my lips with the tip of your tongue.

I licked and lapped her.

Hard.

Slow, then fast building with each stroke.

I gradually slid my fingers into her hot slippery temple.

Gentle at first, but she bounced, bucked and rode.

Her rhythmic frantic hips rotated in and out, up and down.

The muscles in my forearm burned as her pussy yelled and screamed.

She rocked and rode my mouth and fingers.

She detonated while I dinned greedily on her feast.

Shhh….

She quaked beneath my mouth, bursting into unrestrained emotion.

She roared my name while glistening tears dripped down her cheeks.

I slowly gently removed my fingers from the temple of worship.

I watched her radiant sweaty copper skin quiver beneath me.

I listened to her voice tremble and try to form words, and then sentences.

I simply said,

Shhh....I understand.

Stiletto

My beautiful date, exuded grace-filled energy as she emerged from the car.
She glowed and glided in my direction.
Her mystique, her fire, and femininity made me boil and think naughty.
She was quite combustible once she was upon me.
Her jewelry and makeup were flawless, her red dress was tight & fitted,
It made me hungry…I couldn't wait pull it up over her head.
But then I froze when I saw her stilettos.
I stared at her silver stilettos encrusted with thousands of rhinestones.
They were chrome with all these blinding stones.
The heels were high, made of steel, and shimmering with lots of bling, and rhinestones and things.
I felt greedy, like a junkie or a fiend.
Yearning, and drooling while I watched her walk.
I no longer cared about the play, our date or seeing something on Broadway.
I wanted to watch her stilettos while she while she glided along, at this point I wanted to avoid the throng.

I wanted her to mount and ride me wildly,
her lips and tongue all over me.
Watching her walk was like visual masturbation,
Her stilettos communicated illicit visuals of her climbing my face.
Those stilettos made me volatile and flammable.
I tried appearing normal and keeping my composure.
Before we arrived at our orchestra seats, she said escort me to the bathroom.
I thought this is dangerous,
I may burst into flames
I'm going to blow up,
Detonate all over her face.
When she entered the large stall,
She removed her silver thong from around her ankles,
My eyes then focused on her twinkling stilettos.
Gradually she lifted her right leg onto my left shoulder.
She was so hot; she ignited my mouth and we both started to smolder.
I ate her hungrily, plunging my fingers deep in her private sector.
She exploded and gushed like a geyser.

To this day, I think I'm still high on her nectar.

Hardwood Floors

I kneeled on the freezing hardwood floor
as she sat on the edge of the sofa.
I started kissing her toes and feet.
I kissed her ankles and listened while she
whimpered and moaned.
As I kissed her up her legs and inner thighs,
I removed her pink laced panties,
I tried to focus,
but the hard ass floor was killing me.
But I held it together cause I wanted to
eat.
She grabbed my braids and whispered,
"Zee"
I kissed and caressed up to her breast,
as her treasure started calling me.
I licked and flicked her firm nipples,
I kissed her neck then her shoulders while
the floor.
I watched her body's respond with quivers
and flinches to my tiny moist kisses.
I dined on her throbbing prize until she
could take no more.
She erupted, while my bruised knees
banged the hardwood floor.

I Saw You Through the Peephole

It was a cold and windy night, yet I sat there waiting for your arrival.

Many nights our headquarters are dull, boring and dank...until I saw you.

I lingered just to see your risqué beauty.

I waited to see your long muscular legs, the sneaky grin across your face, and those red stilettos.

Sometimes I just waited for the stilettos, but just so you know, I watched you...

I watched you....you and baby dyke, walking hand-in-hand as the wind whipped the trees and made the branches dance.

I still wonder, how old is this little tattooed girl you so eagerly seduce, slurp and kiss after hours in the park?

At times I can hear you swallow, and smack as if drinking the soft wetness of her tongue.

I saw how you straddled her lap when she sat on the grass.

I watched her tiny tattooed baby dyke hands caress your thighs as you began to grind.

I noticed your lips slightly part, and head tilt to the left while your locks covered parts of your face.

I could see your bright red lipstick glistening through the moonlight while her little bitty baby dyke hands unbuttoned your blouse, and unfastened your bra.

I heard the way you whimpered when she flicked your left nipple with her pierced tongue, and pinched the right between her fingertips.

I saw ecstasy on your face when baby dyke's left hand disappeared under your skirt.

I gazed at your lips as you whispered in her ear, guiding her to your hungry spot.

I listened as your soft whispers and moans became shouts of profanity.

You cursed as baby dyke's strokes became pounding thrusts.

Baby dyke's skinny waif-like left forearm disappeared then re-appeared.

It disappeared then re-appeared.

I felt your energy as you rode baby dyke.

I watched you grip baby dyke's shoulders, then her neatly braided hair.

I gasped as multi-colored beads exploded from her braided mane.

I saw you erupt.

I saw you.

I saw you through the peephole.

About Azaan Kamau

Azaan Kamau is a writer, photographer and publisher! She has a diverse mix of charm, intellect, creativity and spirituality. In The midst of all of that, Azaan remains approachable, modest and quite grounded to the people and things that matter. Azaan's optimistic attitude has set her on a path for empowerment of for all people and creeds.

While trying to navigate her personal life, her demanding career, Azaan is quite focused on uplifting and empowering others through poetry, publishing, photography, screen writing and even broadcast media.

"I believe through education, knowledge, and acceptance there is no force that can oppress us" – Azaan

After falling in love with writing, her goal is to give voice to people and topics that have been muted or swept under the rug or even ignored by mainstream society. Azaan's work and commitment has given her a distinguished literary reputation.

Azaan's passion for writing poetry began in the early 1980's! Since then, Azaan has been published in countless publications, and has written numerous volumes of poetry that shock, awe and inspire!

Azaan built Glover Lane Press by hand, one exhausting brick at a time back in the year 2000 with the help of her mentors. To this day, Azaan & Glover Lane Press have published and designed numerous books on various topics, which include eBooks! In addition to Azaan's publishing career, Azaan is a poet, photographer and print media designer that has won several awards!

People also recognize Azaan as one of the prized Outfest Photographers and an artist and in the esteemed Getty Underground global art exhibition. For many years, Azaan's aesthetic eye captivated the Getty Underground audiences at the prestigious Getty Museum in Los Angeles, California.
This award-winning multi-media talent is also known as the former editor of GBF Magazine. GBF Magazine was the first

Black Lesbian Magazine ever distributed globally and was rated # 1 in the country! Azaan wrote for the amazing Susan Webley who birthed Sable Magazine. She wrote for Femnoir.net and also Women In the Life! She is also the former Creative Director of STUD Magazine.

Often people say Azaan is like family! Azaan consistently exudes a warmth, and irresistible charisma that connect with all people and cultures.

Other notable books by Azaan Kamau Include: In the Midst of My Blackness, Ray Charles Robinson; A Love & Romance, Letter's to My Bully, Riveting, Got Homophobia, Your Body Wants to Heal Naturally, The Dank Dictionary, and the ground breaking STUD Dispelling the Myths.

Visit Azaan and Glover Lane Press on Amazon, Facebook or Instagram.

Thank youuuuu!

www.ingramcontent.com/pod-product-compliance
Lightning Source LLC
LaVergne TN
LVHW051204080426
835508LV00021B/2800